Quantum Teaming: A Primer

Teaming in the 21st Century Self-Information Age

Desiree L. DePriest

Copyright © 2016 Desiree L. DePriest
All rights reserved.
ISBN: 1523492309
ISBN-13: 978-1523492305

Dedication

This book is dedicated to Danielle and David who are my twin stars sent to provide creative light and purposeful direction. It is a privilege to share my business, life, and love with you.

CONTENTS

	Acknowledgments	ii
1	Entanglement	1
2	Superposition	Pg 10
3	Uncertainty	Pg 22

Acknowledgements

I would like to recognize all my students and interns who provided an opportunity to explore the quantum teaming experience. I am confident you will all go forth, spread quantum teaming and make me proud.

Welcome to Quantum Teaming: What You Already Know

Chapter One: Understanding Entanglement

The Quantum Teaming Organization
Step One: Entanglement

- Humans entangle innately:
    - Air
    - Gravity
    - Language
    - Body structure and senses
    - Culture
    - Evolving appropriate structures and processes for sharing resources and dealing with challenges in our external environment a.k.a. lifelong learning

What is Quantum Teaming Entanglement?

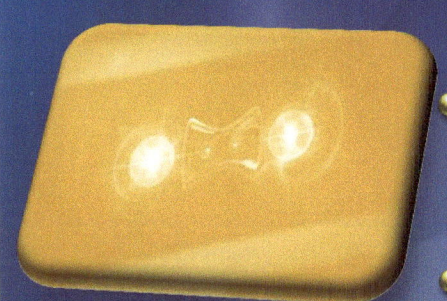

- In every area of life, we observe and are affected by our external environments
- We seek to apply our internal resources through understanding the challenges in our external environment
- Positive entanglement fuses internal and external resources through balanced emphasis on team commitments
- The members' internal resources, or self-information, are equally as important as the organization's external resources
- We call this quantum teaming blending entanglement

QT Entanglement Explained

- Quantum teaming seeks to leverage each member's abilities within the organization
- Quantum teaming states that each adult member enters the organization with previously honed skills or abilities and seeks to utilize them to benefit the whole team
- Quantum teaming states that honed skills from previous experiences are transferrable to any other type of organization
- Quantum teaming flips the traditional team mindset where the new member tries to clone what is already being done
- It encourages entangling the project with the individual team member's innate skills and abilities to lead and leverage what they contribute
- Based on the presenting environment, the member ascertains what makes sense to them based on their experience and wisdom

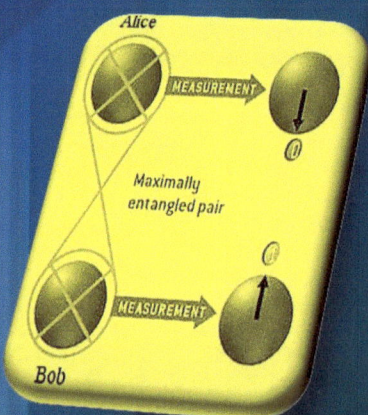

QT Entanglement Process

- Focus is on discovering and welcoming the acquired skills of the incoming team member and supporting those skills
- Member-centric vs. project-centric teams allows for diversification of resources and replenishing of energy through inclusion of the new member's honed skills transferred to the team projects
- QT entanglement offers the member an alternative to the traditional external power-based, top-down constructions in teaming and allows exploration of their own ideas and approaches to achieve the shared goal
- The QT environment embraces diversity, variations and modifications in approaches to success
- This is accomplished through negotiating positive team consensus and then delegating task ownership based on individual strengths

QT Entanglement Approach: Negotiate to Yes

- The *progress* approach in quantum teaming:
    - **I think this is the next best step to take, what do you think?**
    - The traditional approach is, "What do you want me to do next?"
- The *response* approach in quantum teaming:
    - **If I understand correctly, you are suggesting X,Y,Z. Am I understanding you correctly?**
    - The traditional approach is, "I don't think that will work because…"
- The *corrective* approach in quantum teaming:
    - **Good idea. Can we expand on or join that idea with doing X,Y,Z?**
    - The traditional approach is, "I think it would be better to do it a different way."

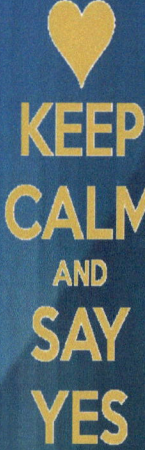

QT Entanglement: Challenges

- Some theorists suggest, if entanglement is innate, the response to the external environment is also innate or a fixed action pattern and therefore unchangeable
- Quantum teaming allows for member-perceptions of the environment to unfold on a spectrum
- A member can evolve, seek tradition or experience entropy within a quantum teaming environment. These are called:
  - Positive, neutral or negative entanglement
  - Neutral entanglement occurs when a member's preference is for traditional teaming.
    - The team provides the member with traditional structures and support while continuing in quantum team entanglement
  - Negative entanglement creates silos (repressed energy) that lead to entropy within the individual and potential chaos within the team.
    - If not correctable, it is the only member-state rejected in quantum teaming
    - It is the antithesis of negotiating to yes

Summary: Entanglement

- Entanglement is a self-realized and then member-recognized choice in team perception.
- Quantum teaming seeks to leverage each intern's abilities within the organization
- Focus is on discovering and welcoming the acquired skills of the incoming team member and supporting those skills
- Quantum teaming states member-perception of the environment is on a spectrum: Positive, neutral or negative
- The QT environment embraces diversity, variations and modifications in approaches to success through negotiating to positive team consensus and then delegation of task ownership based on individual strengths

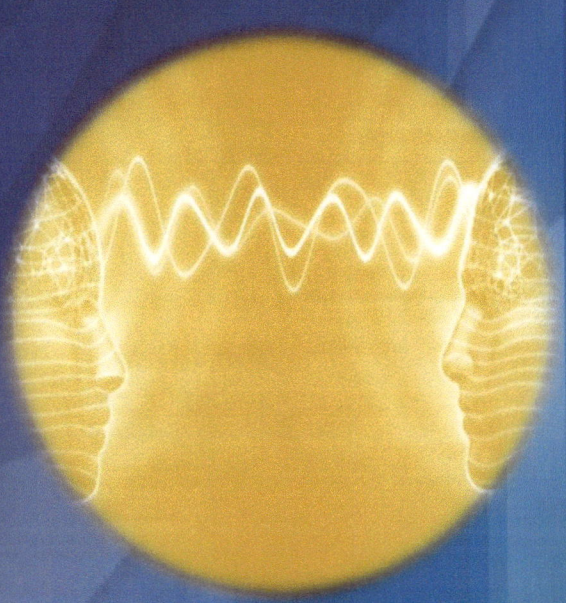

Intentionally Left Blank

Quantum Teaming: You are Energy!

Chapter Two: Understanding Superposition

Quantum Teaming Warm-up

The two basic premises of quantum teaming are:

- Humans naturally **entangle** positively (or otherwise) when placed into teams. This is called sharing a *quantum state*
- Every entangled human is capable of taking a position in life and evolving it into **superposition**

SUPERPOSITION

Quantum Teaming Warm-up

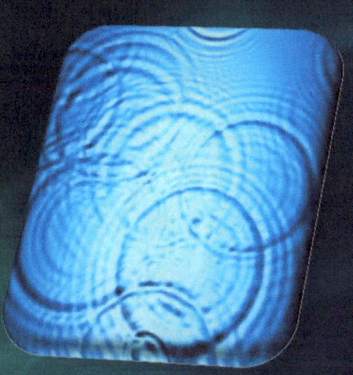

QT EXERCISE: We are not talking about one individual but a team of entangled individuals:

- How does one drop of water become concentric circles of water?
- How does a small team become a successful company?

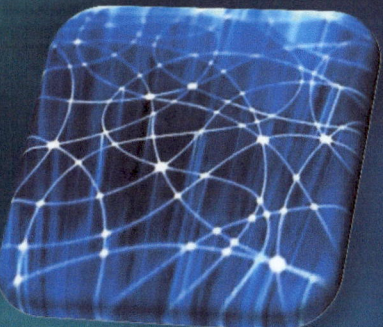

- The answer:

SUPERPOSITION

Quantum Teaming Warm-up

- The same way computer chips can fit on the head of pin but have increased High-Bandwidth Memory (HBM), a quantum team can accomplish more than a traditional team.
- We think about every important aspect of how to make a project succeed.
- We think about performance, mental power efficiency, and new ways of doing things.
- We communicate with our team on aspects of the project we want to own.
- Each individual takes ownership of a part of the project overlapping the team's owners in quantum superposition.
- Quantum Superposition is doing more with less!

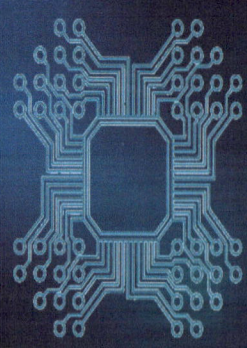

Quantum Teaming Warm-up

- Clark Kent was a passive and introverted personality with conservative mannerisms at a newspaper called "The Daily Planet."
  - But, that was not his true superposition
- Underneath Kent's street clothes (or personality) was Kal-El or Superman who would rise to superposition to help the greater good.
- Superman, along with other super people, went forward to create a team called the Justice League
- The team is only as great as the member's ability to rise to superposition within the quantum team.

The Organization

- Organizations can adapt to their environment and create solutions involving multiple resources:
    - Workers
    - Departments
    - Partnerships
    - Technologies
    - Clients

- These resources can be further classified as independent (external) or dependent (internal).

Organizations Seeking Superposition

- Each business resource has triple constraints (time, current/budget, scope) = Potential Energy
- When each individual contributes to the solutions through engaging one or more resources, we create Active Energy or "adequate or abundant power"
- All resources have *potential energy* but need our entanglement to create *active energy*
    - The level of energy given to any project is up to each individual in the team

You

Independent and Dependent Resources

Independent Example:

- Clients: Clients are free, at any time, to come or go because they are independent of the organization
- To achieve superposition, all clients should be given the same amount of active energy from the departments and/or workers assigned to the contract
- A Work Breakdown Structure and Project Charter should be provided before for client agreement prior to start of all contracts
- Regular status meetings should be provided to the client with copious progress notes and anticipated milestones
- Contact with the client contributes to active energy between resources; active energy creates superposition

Independent and Dependent Resources

Dependent Example:
- Departments: The energy given to projects from each team affects the success of every other team
- If your department is not directly involved in the activities of another team's projects, the indirect energy from each encouraging team maintains the healthy momentum (construct) for the entire organization

Summary: Superposition

- The two basic premises of quantum teaming are:
  - Humans naturally entangle positively (or otherwise) when placed into teams. This is called sharing a quantum state
  - Every entangled human is capable of taking a position in life and evolving it into superposition
- Quantum Superposition is doing more with less!
- The team is only as great as the member's ability to rise to superposition within the quantum team
- Organizations can adapt to their environment and create solutions involving multiple resources:
  - Workers
  - Departments
  - Partnerships
  - Technologies
  - Clients
- All resources have potential energy but need the team to create active energy
  - The level of energy given to any project is up to each individual in the team

Quantum Teaming:

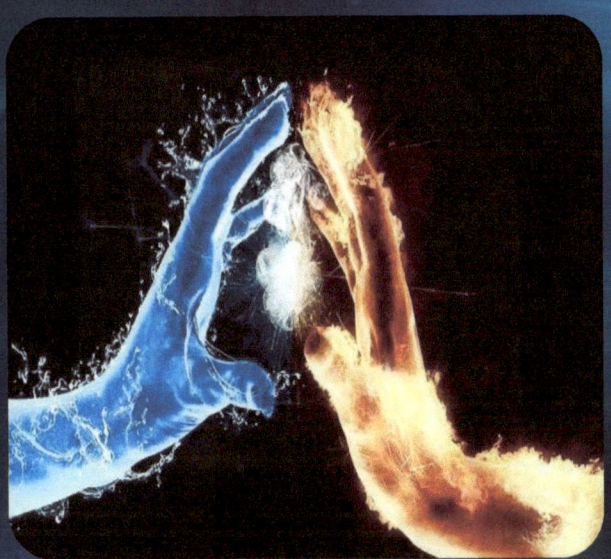

http://www.dalimara.com/blog/1871-what-is-human-energy-field

SUPERPOSITION

Quantum Teaming (QT): You are Here – Or Not!

Chapter Three: Understanding Uncertainty

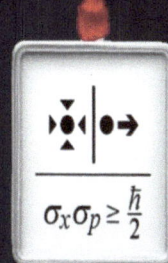

Quantum Teaming
Uncertainty

- Uncertainty in quantum teaming is radically distinct from the familiar notion of risk due to the essential fact that 'risk' *can* have a certain measurement
- QT uncertainty leans toward team projects 'in motion' where discrete random variables are probabilistic but cannot be measured directly
- QT uncertainty applies to teams in non-bureaucratic organizations:
  - Global organizations (with strong virtual components and subcomponents)
  - Non-profit organizations with heavy reliance on volunteers
  - Organic social networking organizations
  - Learning organizations that rely on term-based internships

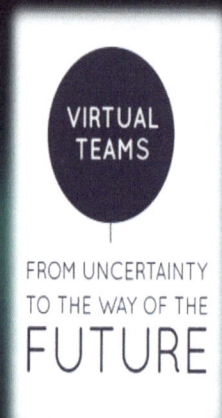

VIRTUAL TEAMS

FROM UNCERTAINTY TO THE WAY OF THE FUTURE

Quantum Teaming Logic in Uncertainty

- Uncertainty itself is not measurable when it is in virtual yet real-time motion. Examples:
    - When a member is seeking to apply a new skill to a project or entangle with a new team, the outcome of these processes are uncertain
- Knowing what happened prior to the member's uncertainty and then measuring the output after uncertainty determines if entanglement and/or superposition have occurred. Examples:
    - Knowing a member recently learned a skill and then observing if that member completed the task successfully using the new skill
    - Knowing a member is new to the team and then observing if that member takes on significant superposition within the team

- The "black box" between member input and output creates a period of uncertainty
- The concepts of the Bayesian Surprise theory are applied in QT through knowing the state of the member *prior* to uncertainty and then measuring the posterior state of the member *after* the period of uncertainty

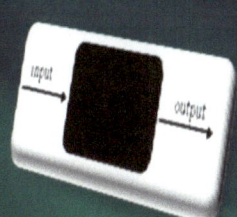

Bayesian Surprise Concept in Uncertainty

- QT applied in organizational environments that are not deterministic or predictable in real-time assumes periods of uncertainty
- If the environment is virtual and further challenged with transitory workers, missing information or skillsets, and limited resources, the uncertainty is increased
- Uncertainty corresponds to each member's:
  - Subjective perceptions of quantum teaming and how that is applied to the objective resources through -
    - Positive entanglement
    - Neutral entanglement
    - Negative entanglement

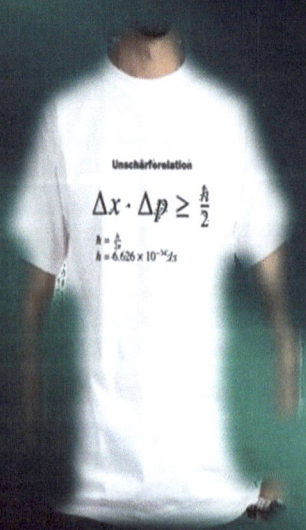

QT Uncertainty and Surprise

- The QT team member whose perception evolves from 1) the prior milestones, 2) adjusts to uncertainty, and then 3) arrives at the posterior end-stop, transforms uncertainty into surprise
- Surprise can be further defined as the satisfaction occurring from successful completion an uncertain task
- A unit of surprise in the Bayesian Surprise theory is called a "Wow."

Recent "Surprise" or "Wow" studies explain that humans are significantly attracted towards surprising locations in video displays. Over 72% of all human saccades (rapid movement of the eye) were targeted to locations predicted to be more surprising than on average.
Learn more at:
http://ilab.usc.edu/publications/doc/Itti_Baldi06nips.pdf

http://ilab.usc.edu/surprise/

Uncertainty and QT Entanglement

- Starting from uncertainty, an experiment measured the rapid movement of the eye between fixed endpoints from four unguided observers watching a video. The results showed that humans preferentially saccaded towards the three active hotspots (each slide in "a" represents an observers' saccade) corresponding to the instantaneous eye positions of the other three humans with near-unity metric responses

- This study suggests, within the uncertainty that occurs in QT environments, humans naturally entangle and demonstrate teaming responses

http://www.ncbi.nlm.nih.gov/pmc/articles/PMC2782645/pdf/nihms-125636.pdf

Adjusting to QT Uncertainty - Applied

- The quantum teaming environment must be reinforced through training
- Knowledge of quantum teaming creates self-information important to the member's understanding of their position and their momentum in applied projects with high levels of uncertainty
- Understanding uncertainty in the QT environment allows members to produce new innovations through

  - Dynamic creativity without the anxiety-producing measurements of traditional, bureaucratic organizations
  - QT supports methods that are designed to be member-centric transferring the honed skills of each member to the projects
  - QT environments allow members to be attracted to uncertainty as a creative learning step toward the "wow" experiences of teaming

  - Accomplishments become shared surprises positively entangled in organizational superposition
  - These accomplishments are celebrated by the whole organizational team

Summary: QT Uncertainty

If the *present* position is clear, the *future* direction is unclear.

If the *future* direction is clear, the *present* postion is unclear.

Quantum Teaming:

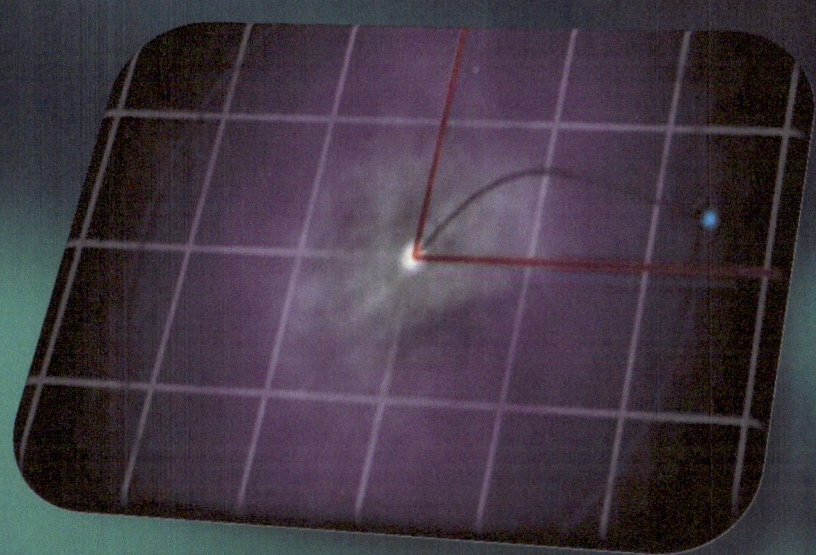

UNCERTAINTY

About The Author

Dr. Desiree L. DePriest is an entrepreneur and university professor in the information technology and instructional design fields. She is a prominent speaker on issues related to virtual learning, change, and new approaches to organizational teams.

Her focus is on creating quantum teaming experiential learning environments where students can apply active and practical business intelligence solutions. The work and its applications are to create business environments with quantum teaming as the key framework for 21st century organizations dealing with the self-information age .

www.ingramcontent.com/pod-product-compliance
Lightning Source LLC
Chambersburg PA
CBHW051112180526
45172CB00002B/873